Appreciate my love :

I need you & I need your love .

# Contents



# Chapter 1: Feelings

## Appreciate my love .

Appreciate my love or leave me alone , appreciate my feelings or just leave me alone . How can I be happy when you are always being negative to me . I'm trying can't you understand!, why do you want me to impress you? . Why is it hard to accept me for who I am ? .

Is it part of my responsibility to accept the situation the way it is and love you while you still hurt me . My feelings are extremely expanding in pain. My plans always land in a wrong land , I can't stop thinking about how much a failure I am .

Feeling sorry for myself won't do good for me . I have to keep pushing until I get what I want . I had to finish my race completely, no excuses . I have a dream like Martin Luther Kings , I have a dream to change the world and why don't you appreciate me like you appreciate people who already change the world. Is it about status ?

If not what is it about ? I feel like I have to impress you to love me . Why can't we just connect for who we are ? . I believe the people out there in the world is waiting for me so we can connect just like my family waited for me to arrive in this world . I can't always be defeated by people who don't understand me and doesn't benefits me at all.

This is a lonely journey, a journey that I will lose most I love , I wish I can atleast have loyal people the end of my journey . If only I could look at it like a book and everytime new adventure there is a new chapter . I have been in one place for a year , I deserve a change in life , I deserve everything that work for and I deserve to be appreciated.

If I were to past on , what will you remember me with ? To be honest

I want everyone to remember me with my drive . I want everyone to remember me with everything I contributed on this earth and I know before I die I'll contribute something that will benefit the future generations.

I never enjoyed my childhood, I felt like I want to leave home . I never been happy home . I just feel like I want to start my own home and with people who really appreciate me for who I am . Sometimes I feel like I should understand them but their actions tells me otherwise. This is my life, my choices and my legacy to build for my children.

I can't let feelings take control and can't people affect my feelings . I have to leave life the way I want to leave it .

All I'm asking for myself is to be patient and believe in myself . I know I can achieve anything I want if I just believe in myself .

This is my time to show myself what I made of , to prove to myself that I can work hard and get anything I put my mind on . It will never be over until I get I want and I know deep down that I will get what I want .

Appreciate me until my
old ages

# Part II

Why is it hard to appreciate every little piece of love I create for you ?

I have a garden that is full of different flowers and blowing winds . I was looking forward if you can come and appreciate life with me there .

I don't normally invite people but I just want you .

Only you! Only for your eyes .

When you accepted my invitation and came.You didn't come alone but with your buddy called betrayal .

You let him sneak him so he can steal my pride .

Why do I have to give you so many chances and what you do it act like you appreciate them so bad but deep down you wish I should have gave you a chance .

Why are you showing me a side that ain't yours ?

Why are you full of betrayal?

Why do you want to destroy me so bad ?

I wish everything you show me can be real .

You seem like a good person indeed but your actions tell me otherwise .

I don't know if we'll reach to the finish line together .

I feel like you are just a distraction to my life .

I wish we could built something that could remind us of all the memories we had .

It's pains me to feel this way , especially always losing over some stupid actions .

I just wish you would have appreciated us at the beginning.

We never been taught how we should fight our pain

This is me learning and accepting everything.

I influenced the world because without me everything will be different.

I will take responsibility for your wrong as I know you lacked knowledge.

If I have a problem with the world I'll change the world myself .
Everything is my fault.
I'll make this world a better place whether you appreciate me or not .

It's okay to take a break
#help

# I AM IN PAIN!

I am In pain of understanding my
own thoughts.
Amend me with my true thoughts.
My mind and soul have retired from
my body
I am tired of fighting my own family
No one can save me from these
mystery illness
Please save me from this illness
African doctors demands more than
I can offer
I don't want to die sad

No one understands how painful I feel and no one care that's too sad .

It's okay to take a break

## Abuse Me

Abuse me as you want , you never
cared about my feelings .

Break my bones like animal , we
both know you don't care about my
feelings

I'm really tired of you

I'm tired of you,controlling me

I'm really tired of you

I'm tired of you , bulling me .

I feel scared and weak around you .

I'm scared to call you my husband

I can't believe you are the man who
is abusing me , a man who treat me
like a punching bag and I can't
believe you are my husband .

7 years of this marriage and I became your slave .

Why don't you change my title from a wife to a slave .

I can't take this anymore I feel like I want to die .

I love you so much , I can't choice to leave you and be with Someone else . I can't picture my soul with someone else , I just want to die .

What change between us ?

What can we between us?

I'm asking , I'm willing to do what It takes for us . Can't you understand that I love you so much .

Can't you understand that I'm willing to do anything for us .I want to spend my whole life with you . I'm just tired of you abusing me . I just want to be your wife and love you forever .These abuse and fights are hurting me so much .

All I'm asking is peace and harmony. I tried to find help so people can talk to us but it didn't help

You felt embarrassed and angry because you believe no one can teach you how to drive your own family .

The abuse became worse and the children started to witness how their father abuse their mother .

The mother's curse was transfer to her children .

I couldn't take it anymore, I couldn't stand there and see my children get abused daily .

Yes I finally did it , I took my children and left .

It was really hard to do so ,It was hard to leave him . My life without him was nothing and I saw light .

My life is my children and myself .I choose me over love and safety .

I'll find love somewhere I'm appreciated.

WOMEN HAVE RIGHTS
GIRLS JUST WANNA HAVE FUNDAMENTAL HUMAN RIGHTS

WOMEN'S RIGHTS
ARE
HUMAN RIGHTS

# I'm just a child

I'm just a child , I don't deserve to be treated like a slave .
I know I have to depend on my parents In the mean while but I'm not anyone slave .
I feel like I'm not understood
I splash feelings and thoughts to all of you and still I'm not understood .
I don't deserve to be treated like I don't belong here which is home .
I really feel alone , I feel like I don't have a home .

I just want to feel alive and happy .

Why can't I just be happy ?

For moment I thought I was happy .

Teach me how to survive so I can understand and be independent.

The love to the child is teaching them how to be independent when a parents is no longer there for them . I just want you to teach me how to independent

#help

# Chapter 2 : Matters

<u>Rose and Sunlight .</u>

I appreciate that rose I always get when I go to a romantic date with you .

Now I don't receive it anymore

I appreciate those roses you would deliver to my house when I'm mad at you .

Now I don't receive it anymore.

I wish my current partner can just appreciate me like you do .

Now outside listening to the heat from the sunlight .

I'm thinking deeper than ever perhaps I'm lost since you not here with me .

I hear voices coming from the sunlight rays , telling me that it's not too late to go back to him .

I'm sure he's feeling the same way as I'm feeling .

Maybe he's better without me . I took his love and played him . He told me that one day I'll miss him but I never believed him .

Now I can't smell any roses from my hands .

Why do I have to learn the hard way
?
I wish I can go back and change things .
I wish I could at least appreciate you and every little thing especially the roses .
Now I don't receive it anymore
I feel lonely without you
Can you at-least call me
I'm so desperate to see you and I'm starting feel like I'm a psycho .

# Hold My heart

Hold my heart safe deep down the core of the earth lava .

I carried you for 9 months and this is your time to show me your love .

I raised you with pride and a lot of sacrifices .

Please don't let me down , do whatever it takes to get what you want . Take risk and make sacrifices.

Hold my heart as these is my last breath.

Don't forget what I taught you son , whatever you focus on requires strengths .

The world is full of too much mysterious things so pray everyday so God can guide you.

I fought so many wars for you .

Tell my grandchildren about me and never forget the love I gave you as a mother .

I'm sorry I wasn't there every-time you need me but I was always there for you as a mother .

Pray for opportunities, safety, strength and knowledge my son .I'll forever be in your heart .

This world is full of temptation, we all choose the temptation that can defeat our heart .

Choose your losses wisely and choose failures wisely .

What I mean is we all going to fail at sometime in our lives so I advise you to choose where you going to fail wisely .

If you not comfortable in that position of failure , continue to strive to the comfortable position you desire .

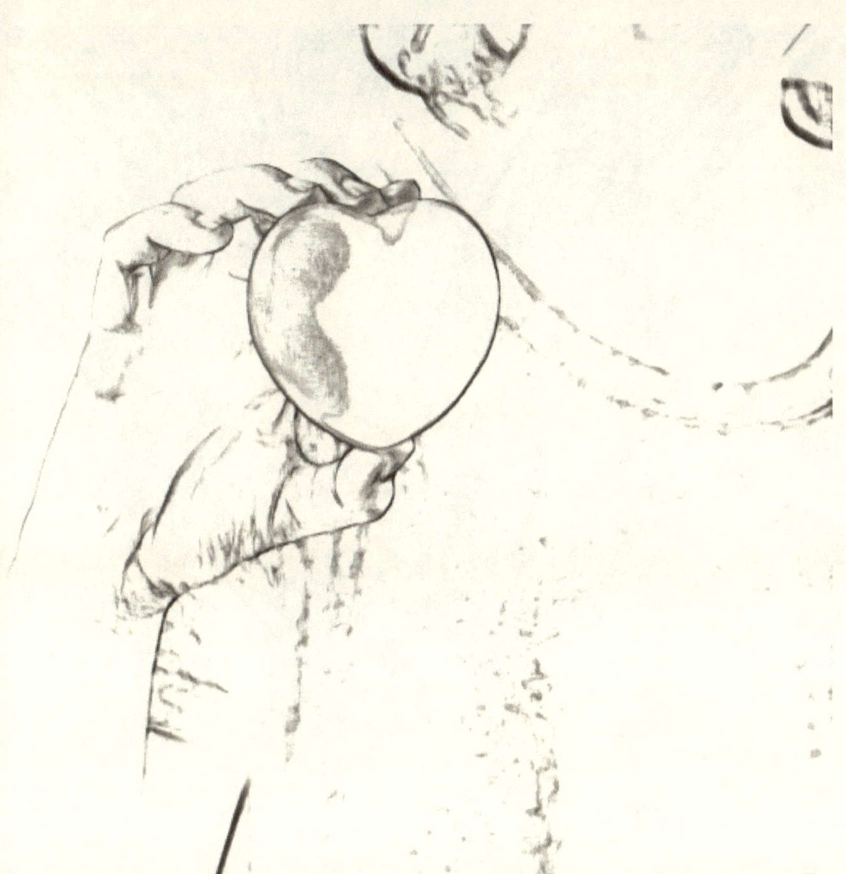

# Child Abuse helpline

# Germany

Ludwigshafen, Germany
**Website**
http://www.saferinternet.de[1]

---

# About the organisation

The German Safer Internet Centre (SIC DE) exists to promote a safer and better use of the internet and mobile technologies among children and young people.

*Profile last updated: March 2022*

# Awareness centre

Description:

klicksafe aims to promote people's online competence and to support them with a wide range of services to help them use the internet competently and critically. On the website, users can find a wealth of up-to-date information, practical tips and teaching material on digital services and topics. The target groups are teachers, educators, parents, children, young people and multipliers.

klicksafe is politically and economically independent and is implemented by the Media Authority of Rhineland-Palatinate (coordinator) and the State Media Authority of North Rhine-Westphalia.

The key platform www.klicksafe.de[1] offers access to the whole portfolio of materials.

Email address: info@klicksafe.de

Website: http://www.klicksafe.de[2]

Social media:

https://www.facebook.com/klicksafe

https://twitter.com/klicksafe

https://www.youtube.com/user/

klicksafegermanyhttps://www.instagram.com/klicksafe

---

1. http://www.klicksafe.de/

2. http://www.klicksafe.de/

# Helpline

Description:

Nummer gegen Kummer e.V. (NgK) is the umbrella organisation of the largest toll-free and anonymous counselling service for children, adolescents, parents and other carers in Germany and looks back on 40 years of experience as a general helpline.

Since 2008, NgK is the national helpline within the German Safer Internet Centre (SIC). Young people can call the Child helpline at 116111 (peer-to-peer counselling on Saturdays) or contact the online counselling services (chat, e-mail) via the website www.nummergegenkummer.de[1]. The parent's helpline can be reached via 0800 – 111 0 550.

The helpline is open to all topics, including online safety issues, and offers a safe place to talk, seek advice, comfort or simply a sympathetic ear. NgK's trained volunteer counsellors support those seeking advice to find their own solutions (by helping them to help themselves). If needed, counsellors can provide information about specialised/professional help or recommend relevant (online) sources of information enabling young people or parents to further educate themselves.

Email address: info@nummergegenkummer.de

Website: https://www.nummergegenkummer.de[2]

Social media:

https://www.facebook.com/ngk.dachverband

---

1. https://www.nummergegenkummer.de/

2. https://www.nummergegenkummer.de/

https://www.youtube.com/c/
NummergegenKummereVhttps://www.instagram.com/
nummergegenkummer_e.v

# Hotline

Description:

The German Safer Internet Centre (SIC) has two national alert platforms for reporting of illegal content on the internet, particularly in respect of child pornography, racism and xenophobia: IBSDE[1], operated by the hotlines of eco and FSM as independent partners, and jugendschutz.net[2].

As a consortium set up by the partners eco and FSM, IBSDE is 'industry driven' and has a self-regulatory approach. eco is the Internet Service Providers Association in Germany and represents organisations of the (German) internet industry, as well as all enterprises that make commercial use of the internet. FSM is the German non-profit association for voluntary self-regulation in online and mobile media and was founded by numerous media associations and media enterprises. Its members are media and telecommunications organisations, as well as companies who offer their products and services online.

jugendschutz.net is a government institution and was established as an initiative of the Youth Ministers of the German Federal States. As a competence centre for the protection of minors on the internet, jugendschutz.net looks closely at risks in services specifically attractive to young users. Risky contacts, self-harm behaviour, political extremism and the sexual exploitation of children is the focus of jugendschutz.net's work.

---

1. https://www.internet-beschwerdestelle.de/

2. https://jugendschutz.net/

The hotline partners are collaborating closely, for example by regular meetings, exchange of expertise and participation in joint projects.
The hotline website addresses are:
www.fsm.de/de[3]
www.eco.de[4]
beschwerdestelle.eco.de[5]
www.jugendschutz.net[6]
www.internet-beschwerdestelle.de[7]
The hotline email addresses are:
office@fsm.de
hotline@eco.de
buero@jugendschutz.net
Social media:
https://www.facebook.com/fsm.de/
https://twitter.com/FSM_de
https://www.youtube.com/user/FSMBerlinhttps://twitter.com/eco_politik

---

3. http://www.fsm.de/de

4. https://www.eco.de/

5. http://beschwerdestelle.eco.de/

6. http://www.jugendschutz.net/

7. http://www.internet-beschwerdestelle.de/

# Youth participation

Description:

The klicksafe Youth Panel consists of a group of students concerned with digital trends and relevant issues of the online world. As media scouts, they help younger students navigate through the digital universe via talks on Facebook, WhatsApp and more. Since January 2009, klicksafe has coordinated a cooperative Youth Panel with representatives from different secondary schools.

Information on the Youth Panel is available on the klicksafe website[1].

Email address: rack@medienanstalt-rlp.de

---

1. https://www.klicksafe.de/ueber-klicksafe/die-initiative/project-information-en/youth-und-childrens-panel-english/youth-panel-introduction/

# United state of American

If you would like more information on child abuse, need assistance reporting abuse, or to speak with a Childhelp counselor, please call or text the Childhelp National Child Abuse Hotline at **1-800-4-A-CHILD (1-800-422-4453). You can also live chat with a trained counselor at www.childhelphotline.org**[1]. The hotline is available 24 hours a day and all calls are confidential. For more information on the hotline, visit www.childhelp.org/hotline[2].

If you are contacting Childhelp to receive assistance in reporting abuse, **please do not use the email option below**. Please call or text the Childhelp National Child Abuse Hotline at **1-800-4-A-CHILD (1-800-422-4453). You can also live chat with a trained counselor at www.childhelphotline.org**[3]. While the hotline is available 24 hours a day, email inquiries have a 24-48 hour response time (Monday-Friday). Additionally, emails are not confidential.

For media inquiries and communications, please email Daphne Young at dyoung@childhelp.org or contact her by phone at (480) 922-8212 ext. 446.

For recurring gift inquiries please contact gifts@childhelp.org.

---


1. http://www.childhelphotline.org/

2. https://www.childhelp.org/hotline/

3. http://www.childhelphotline.org/

# Canada

## Childhelp National Child Abuse Hotline[1]

1-800-4ACHILD or 1-800-422-4453 | TDD: 1-800-2A-CHILD. 24/7 - Call from: USA, Canada, Puerto Rico, Guam or the Virgin Islands. - can help in 170 languages. All calls are confidential.

## Operation Come Home[2]

Toll-Free 1 800 668 4663 | Local 613 230 4663 - 8am-4pm Monday to Friday.

---

1. http://www.childhelp.org/get_help

2. http://operationcomehome.ca/programs/reunite/

# Swiss

SWAGAA[1] - + 268 505 7514

---

1. https://www.facebook.com/Swaziland-Action-Group-Against-Abuse-SWAGAA-202248446510926/

# South Africa

Childline SouthAfrica[1] - 0800 055 555

---

1. http://www.childlinesa.org.za/

# Women abuse helpline

# Germany

1. National Emergency Hotline: 911. Aleng Pulis Hotline: 0919 777 7377. ...

# United state of American

The Office on Violence Against Women reduces violence against women. They help victims of domestic violence, dating violence, sexual assault, and stalking.

**Acronym:**

OVW

**Website:**

Office on Violence Against Women[1]

**Contact:**

Contact the Office on Violence Against Women[2]

**Local Offices:**

Find help near you[3]

---

1. https://www.justice.gov/ovw

2. https://www.justice.gov/ovw/contact-ovw

**Main Address:**

U.S. Department of Justice
Office on Violence Against Women
145 N Street, NE, Suite 10W.121
Washington, DC 20530

**Email:**

ovw.info@usdoj.gov

**Phone Number:**

1-202-307-6026

**Toll Free:**

1-800-799-7233 (Domestic Violence Hotline)
1-800-656-4673 (Sexual Assault Hotline)
1-866-331-9474 (Teen Dating Abuse Helpline)
1-855-484-2846 (Victim Hotline)

**TTY:**

1-202-307-2277
1-800-787-3224 (Domestic Violence Hotline)
1-866-331-8453 (Teen Dating Abuse Helpline)

---

3. https://www.justice.gov/ovw/local-resources

# Australia

# IF YOU ARE AT RISK

If you, or someone you know, is in immediate danger, call 000.

## NATIONAL

### 1800RESPECT
### (1800 737 732)

The National Sexual Assault, Family & Domestic Violence Counselling Line for any Australian who has experienced, or is at risk of, family and domestic violence and/or sexual assault.

24 hours, 7 days a week.

www.1800respect.org.au[1]

### Lifeline
### (13 11 14)

A national number which can help put you in contact with a crisis service in your state.

24 hours, 7 days a week.

www.lifeline.org.au[2]

## AUSTRALIAN CAPITAL TERRITORY

### Domestic Violence Crisis Service (DVCS)
### (02 6280 0900)

Crisis intervention and counselling, family violence intervention program, education and information for the community.

24 hours, 7 days a week.

www.dvcs.org.au[3]

---

1. https://www.1800respect.org.au/

2. https://www.lifeline.org.au/

3. https://dvcs.org.au/

## Canberra Rape Crisis Centre (CRCC)
## (02 6247 2525)

Crisis support, counselling advocacy and support programs for men and women.
7am -10.30pm
On call for ACT Health and Police
www.crcc.org.au[4]

# NEW SOUTH WALES

## NSW Domestic Violence Line
## (1800 656 463 / TTY 1800 671 442)

Provides telephone counselling, information and referrals for women and same-sex partners who are experiencing or have experienced domestic violence.
24 hours, 7 days a week.
www.community.nsw.gov.au[5]

## NSW Rape Crisis
## (1800 424 017)

Provides telephone and online counselling for anyone who is or has experienced sexual violence and their supporters,
24 hours, 7 days a week.
www.rape-dvservices.org.au[6]

# NORTHERN TERRITORY

## Catherine Booth House
## (8981 5928)

Short term crisis accommodation, referral and support for adult and young women over 18 years old.
24 hours, 7 days a week.
www.shelterme.org.au[7]

## Darwin Aboriginal and Islander Women's Shelter (DAIWS)
## (08 8945 2284)

---

4. http://www.crcc.org.au/

5. https://www.facs.nsw.gov.au/families

6. https://www.rape-dvservices.org.au/

7. https://www.shelterme.org.au/

Support, referral, outreach and domestic violence crisis accomodation for Aboriginal and Torres Strait Islander women who are homeless or escaping family violence.
24 hours, 7 days a week.

## Dawn House (Darwin)
## (08 8945 1388)

Crisis accomodation and support service for women with children who are experiencing or escaping domestic or family violence.
24 hours, 7 days a week.
www.dawnhouse.org.au[8]

## Ruby Gaea (Darwin)
## (08 8945 0155)

Free counselling and support to women and children who have experience sexual assault at any time in their life.
Monday – Friday 8.30am to 5pm.
www.rubygaea.net.au[9]

## Sexual Assault Referral Centre (Darwin)
## (08 8922 6472)

Free 24-hour emergency service that provids crisis counselling and other support needs to both adult and children who have experienced any form of sexual assault or sexual abuse, either recently or in the past.
24 hours, 7 days a week.
www.health.nt.gov.au/sexual_assault_services[10]

## Sexual Assault Referral Centre (Alice Springs)
## (08 8955 4500)

Free 24-hour emergency service that provids crisis counselling and other support needs to both adult and children who have experienced any form of sexual assault or sexual abuse, either recently or in the past.
24 hours, 7 days a week.
www.health.nt.gov.au/sexual_assault_services[11]

# QUEENSLAND

---

8. https://www.dawnhouse.org.au/

9. http://www.rubygaea.net.au/

10. https://nt.gov.au/wellbeing/hospitals-health-services/sexual-assault-referral-centres

11. https://nt.gov.au/wellbeing/hospitals-health-services/sexual-assault-referral-centres

## DVConnect Womensline
## (1800 811 811)

Free state wide telephone service that provides confidential counselling and referral to crisis accommodation for women and children affected by domestic or family Violence and those who are concerned about a friend or family member.

24 hours, 7 days a week.

www.dvconnect.org/womensline[12]

## DVConnect Mensline
## (1800 600 636)

Free state wide telephone service that provides counselling and referral for men for a range of issues especially those who have experienced or use domestic and family violence and those who are concerned about a friend or family member.

9am – 12 midnight, 7 days a week.

www.dvconnect.org/mensline[13]

## DVConnect Sexual Assault Helpline
## (1800 010 120)

Telephone service that provides counselling to women, men and young people who have experienced or are concerned someone they know has experienced sexual assault or abuse.

7.30am – 11.30pm, 7 days a week.

dvconnect.org/queensland-sexual-assault-helpline/[14]

# SOUTH AUSTRALIA

## Domestic Violence and Aboriginal Family Violence Gateway Services
## (1800 800 098)

Counselling and support for women experiencing domestic and family violence.

24 hours, 7 days a week.

womenssafetyservices.com.au[15]

## Yarrow Place Rape and Sexual Assault Services
## (1800 817 421)

---

12. http://www.dvconnect.org/womensline/

13. http://www.dvconnect.org/mensline/

14. http://www.dvconnect.org/queensland-sexual-assault-helpline/

15. http://womenssafetyservices.com.au/

(After hours and emergency 08 8226 8787)

Lead public health agency responding to adult rape and sexual assault in South Australia for people aged 16 years and over.

24 hours, 7 days a week.

www.sahealth.sa.gov.au[16]

# TASMANIA

## Safe at Home Family Violence Response and Referral Line (1800 633 937)

Tasmanian information and referral service where callers are able to access the full range of response, counselling, information and other support services provided by Safe at Home.

24 hours, 7 days a week.

www.safeathome.tas.gov.au[17]

## Family Violence Counselling and Support Service (1800 608 122)

Family Violence Counselling and Support Service offers professional and specialised services to assist children, young people and adults affected by family violence.

9am to midnights weekdays and 4pm to midnight weekends and public holidays.

www.dhhs.tas.gov.au[18]

# VICTORIA

## Safe Steps Family Violence Response Centre (1800 015 188)

Victorian statewide service providing telephone support, information, referral, safety planning and risk assessment for women and children experiencing family violence.

24 hours, 7 days a week.

www.safesteps.org.au[19]

## Sexual Assault Crisis Line (1800 806 292)

A statewide confidential, telephone crisis counselling service for people who have experienced both past and recent sexual assault.

---

16. https://www.sahealth.sa.gov.au/wps/wcm/connect/Public+Content/SA+Health+Internet/Services/
   Primary+and+Specialised+Services/Sexual+Health+Services/Yarrow+Place/Yarrow+Place

17. https://www.safeathome.tas.gov.au/

18. https://www.dhhs.tas.gov.au/

19. https://www.safesteps.org.au/

24 hours, 7 days a week.
www.sacl.com.au[20]

# WESTERN AUSTRALIA

## Women's Domestic Violence Helpline (1800 007 339)

Statewide service providing support and counselling for women experiencing family and domestic violence.

24 hours, 7 days a week.

## Sexual Assault Resource Centre

## 1800 199 888

Statewide service providing emergency services and counselling for people who have experienced both past and recent sexual assault.

https://www.kemh.health.wa.gov.au/Our-services/Statewide-Services/SARC

---

20. http://www.sacl.com.au/

# Cananda

**Ontario**
**Assaulted Women's Helpline:** Provides anonymous and confidential crisis counseling, informational and emotional support to women. (Toronto, ON)
http://www.awhl.org/
Toll Free: 1-866-863-0511
Toll Free TTY: 1-866-863-7868
**Talk for Healing:** Talk4Healing is a helpline available to all Aboriginal women living in urban, rural and remote communities, both on and off reserve, throughout Northern Ontario.
http://www.talk4healing.com/
Telephone: 1-855-554-4325
**Mental Health Crisis Line:** A 24/7 helpline to assist people experiencing a mental health problem or crisis. (Ottawa, ON)
http://www.crisisline.ca/home.htm
Telephone: 613-722-6914
Toll Free: 1-866-996-0991
**Fem'aide:** Provincial helpline for francophone women in Ontario dealing with violence
http://www.femaide.ca/
Telephone: 1-877-336-2433
TTY: 1-866-860-7082
**British Columbia**
**Battered Women's Support Services:** Provides education, advocacy and support services to assist women. (Vancouver, BC)
http://www.bwss.org/
Crisis line: 604-687-1867
Toll Free: 1-855-687-1868
**Greater Vancouver Crisis Line:** Non-profit organizing that provides emotional support to youth, adults and seniors in distress. (Greater Vancouver, BC)
Telephone: 604-872-3311

Toll Free: 1-866-661-3311
TTY: 1-866-872-0113
**Domestic Violence Helpline (Victim Link):** Helpline designed to provide information and support to those experiencing domestic violence.
http://www.domesticviolencebc.ca/
Phone: 604-875-0885
Toll Free TTY: 1-800-563-0808
**Surrey Women's Center:** Offer a range of crisis services to victims of domestic violence, sexual assault, child abuse and other forms of family violence. 24/7 helpline services provided. (Surrey, BC)
http://surreywomenscentre.ca/
Telephone: 604-583-1295
**WAVAW:** Works to end violence against women through various support programs and services including an emotional and informational support 24-hour crisis line.
http://www.wavaw.ca/
24-Hour Crisis Line: 604-255-6344
Toll free: 1-877-392-7583
**North Shore Crisis Services Society:** NSCSS is a transition house and also provides related support services. (North Vancouver, BC)
http://nscss.net/
Telephone: 604-987-3374
**BC Coalition to Eliminate Abuse of Seniors:** Helpline providing emotional and legal information and referral for seniors experiencing abuse. (Vancouver, BC)
http://bcceas.ca/
Telephone: 604-437-1940
Toll free: 1-866-437-1940
TTY: 604-428-3359
TTY Toll free: 1-855-306-1443
**Alberta**
**Crisis Association of Vegreville:** General helpline for those experiencing a problem and require assistance. (Vegreville, Alberta)
Telephone: 1-780-632-2233
Toll Free Helpline: 1-780-632-7070
**Family Violence Info Line:** 24/7 helpline in over 170 languages to provide support and advice for people experiencing family violence.
Telephone: 780- 310-1818
**Edmonton Women's Shelter Ltd.:** A non-profit agency with three shelters for women with or without children leaving domestic violence situations. A 24 hour support and information line is provided. (Edmonton, AB)

http://www.winhouse.org/

Telephone: 780-479-0058

**St. Paul's Crisis Center**: Non-profit organization that provides safe and supportive environments for women with or without children who are experiencing family violence. 24/7 crisis line available for information and emotional support. (St. Paul, AB)

http://www.stpaulcrisiscentre.ca/

Telephone: 645-5195

Toll Free: 1-800-263-3045

**Camrose Women's Shelter Society**: Women's shelter proving safe environments for women and children needing protection from family violence. 24 hour crisis line for additional assistance. (Camrose, AB)

http://brigantiaplace.org/

Phone: 780-672-1035 (main line)

Toll Free Crisis Line: 1-877-672-1010

**Calgary Women's Emergency Shelter**: Offers support to individuals and families fleeing family violence and abuse. The 24-hour helpline provides support, information and access to programs at the shelter. (Calgary, AB)

http://www.calgarywomensshelter.com/home

Telephone: 403-234-7233

Toll Free: 1 (866) 606-7233

**Sucker Creek Women's Emergency Shelter**: Provides range of services for women and children experiencing abuse and assault including a 24-hour crisis line.(Edmonton, AB)

Telephone: 780-523-2929

Crisis Phone: 780-523-4357

Toll Free: 1-866-523-2929

**Saskatchewan**

**La Ronge 24-Hour Crisis Line**: General crisis line for men and women in crisis in La Ronge, Saskatchewan. (La Ronge, SK)

Crisis Line: 306-425-4090

**Moose Jaw Domestic Violence Crisis Line**: Moose Jaw offers a transition house for women and children affected by family violence and abuse. The crisis line offers 24-hour emotional, informational and referral support to women. (Moose Jaw, SK)

http://www.mj-transitionhouse.com/

Hotline: 306-693-6511

**Prince Albert Domestic Violence Crisis Intervention**: General crisis line for those experiencing domestic violence. (Prince Albert, SK)

Crisis Line: 306-764-1011

**Yorkton Domestic Violence Crisis Line**: General crisis line for those experiencing domestic violence in Yorkton. (Yorkton, SK)
Crisis Line: 1-888-783-3111
(Regina) Crisis/Suicide Line: Provides 24-hour social and health crisis response to community of Regina. (Regina, SK)
http://www.mobilecrisis.ca/
Telephone: 306-757-0127
Crisis Line: 306-525-5333
**Manitoba**
**Toll-Free Province Wide Domestic Abuse Crisis Line (24 hours)**: General crisis line for people experiencing domestic violence and abuse in the province of Manitoba.
Toll Free: 1-877-977-0007
**Klinic Crisis Line:** Offers confidential counseling, support and referral to people in crisis.
http://www.klinic.mb.ca/
Crisis Line: (204) 786-8686
Toll free: 1-888-322-3019
TTY (204) 784-4097
**Northwest Territories**
**NWT Help Line:** General helpline there to provide support to those in crisis.
Telephone: 1-800-661-0844
**Nunavut**
**Nunavut Kamatsiaqtut Help Line:** Provides anonymous and confidential counseling for northerners in crisis.
http://www.nunavuthelpline.ca/
Telephone: 867-979-3333
Toll Free: 1-800-265-3333
**Quebec**
**Domestic Violence Hotline:** Provides anonymous and confidential domestic violence services via telephone or email. (Montreal, QC)
www.sosviolenceconjugale.ca
Telephone: 514-873-9010
Toll free: 1-800-363-9010
**Newfoundland**
**Hope Haven Transition House Crisis Line:** Provides confidential and safe emergency shelter to women and children who are experiencing violence and abuse. 24-hour crisis line offers information, emergency planning and emotional support. (Labrador City, NL)
http://www.hopehaven.ca/

Crisis Line: (709) 944-6900
Toll Free: 1-888-332-0000
**Nova Scotia**
**Helpline:** General helpline for people experiencing crisis in Nova Scotia.
Toll Free: 1-877-521-1188
TTY: 1-855-443-2660
**Yukon**
**Kaushee's Place / Yukon Women's Transition Home:** Offers shelter, outreach, support and advocacy for women and their children fleeing abuse.
http://www.womensdirectorate.gov.yk.ca/shelters.html
Crisis Line: 867-668-5733 (collect calls accepted from outside Whitehorse)
Telephone: 867-633-7720

# Swiss

**For persons affected by violence**
In an emergency
Police: www.polizei.ch, tel. 117
Medical assistance: www.erstehilfe.ch, tel. 144


**Information on and addresses of free, confidential and anonymous advice units throughout Switzerland**
www.opferhilfe-schweiz.ch


**Addresses of shelters**
https://opferhilfe-schweiz.ch/de/was-ist-opferhilfe/schutz/
www.frauenhaus-schweiz.ch


**For perpetrators of violence**
Addresses for advice and training programmes:
www.fvgs.ch

---

**Address for enquiries**
Federal Office for Gender Equality
Schwarztorstrasse 51
3003 Bern

---

**Publisher**
Federal Office for Gender Equality
https://www.ebg.admin.ch/ebg/en/home.html [1]

General Secretariat FDHA
http://www.edi.admin.ch [2]

---

1. https://www.ebg.admin.ch/ebg/en/home.html

2. http://www.edi.admin.ch/

# South African

**Women Abuse – Call: ? <u>0800 150 150</u>**

# Depression/suicidal helplines
## Germany

+49 176 62371658[1]

Gotenstraße 74, 10829 Berlin, Germany[2]

1. https://www.google.co.za/

   search?q=germany+mental+health+services&client=safari&hl=en-
   za&sxsrf=ALiCzsbxql9UBb4y9hizPNw08PGGHDf8Mw%3A1653960985469&ei
   =GXGVYqWiHJiO8gLtqICQBQ&oq=germany+depression%2Fsuicide+helpline
   +for+german+citizens&gs_lcp=ChNtb2JpbGUtZ3dzLXdpei1zZXJwEAEYATIH
   CCMQsAMQJzIHCAAQRxCwAzIHCAAQRxCwAzIHCAAQRxCwAzIHCA
   AQRxCwAzIHCAAQRxCwAzIHCAAQRxCwAzIHCAAQRxCwAzIHCAAQ
   RxCwA0oECEEYAFAAWABg-
   jVoAXAAeACAAQCIAQCSAQCYAQDIAQnAAQE&sclient=mobile-gws-wiz-
   serp

2. https://www.google.co.za/

   search?q=germany+mental+health+services&client=safari&hl=en-
   za&sxsrf=ALiCzsbxql9UBb4y9hizPNw08PGGHDf8Mw%3A1653960985469&ei
   =GXGVYqWiHJiO8gLtqICQBQ&oq=germany+depression%2Fsuicide+helpline
   +for+german+citizens&gs_lcp=ChNtb2JpbGUtZ3dzLXdpei1zZXJwEAEYATIH
   CCMQsAMQJzIHCAAQRxCwAzIHCAAQRxCwAzIHCAAQRxCwAzIHCA
   AQRxCwAzIHCAAQRxCwAzIHCAAQRxCwAzIHCAAQRxCwAzIHCAAQ
   RxCwA0oECEEYAFAAWABg-

jVoAXAAeACAAQCIAQCSAQCYAQDIAQnAAQE&sclient=mobile-gws-wiz-serp

# United States of America

The **National Suicide Prevention Lifeline** is a United States-based suicide prevention[1] network of over 160 crisis centers that provides 24/7 service[2] via a toll-free hotline with the number **1 (800) 273-8255 (TALK)**. It is available to anyone in suicidal crisis or emotional distress

1. https://en.m.wikipedia.org/wiki/Suicide_prevention

2. https://en.m.wikipedia.org/wiki/24/7_service

# Australian

Every 30 seconds, a person in Australia reaches out to Lifeline for help. We are a national charity providing all Australians experiencing emotional distress with access to 24 hour crisis support and suicide prevention services.
Call 13 11 14

# Canada

https://www.crisisservicescanada.ca/call-us/

# South Africa

Call :0800567567

# Swiss

https://www.143.ch/

# Drug abusing counseling contact

## (Germany)

**Altona**

**KDROBS Altona, Hohenesch 13-17, 22765 Hamburg, Phone: 040/3908640/ -41, Email: altona@kodrobs.de, Mon, Tue & Thu: 10 a.m. - 7 p.m., ENG**

**Kajal Frauenperspektiven, Substance abuse counselling for women, Haubachstraße 78, 22767 Hamburg, Phone: 040/ 3806987, Email: kajal@frauenperspektiven.de, Mon, Wed, Thu & Fri: 9 a.m. - 5 p.m., Tue: 2:30 p.m. - 5 p.m. Sat: 12 p.m. - 5 p.m., ENG & FR**

**Lukas Suchthilfezentrum, Luruper Hauptstr. 138, 22547 Hamburg, Phone: 040/ 970770, Mon & Thu: 9 a.m. - 6 p.m., Tue & Wed: 10 a.m. - 6 p.m., Fri: 10 a.m. - 3 p.m., ENG**

Palette Bartelsstraße 12, 20357 Hamburg, Phone: 040/ 4302590, Email: bartesstrasse@palette-hamburg.de, Mon - Fri: 11 a.m. - 4 p.m., ENG, FA

**Bergedorf**

KODROBS Bergedorf, Lohbrügger Landstraße 6, 21031 Hamburg, Phone: 040/ 72160-38/ -39, Email: bergedorf@kodrobs.de, Mon, Tue & Fri: 10 a.m. - 5 p.m., Thu: 10 a.m. - 7 p.m.,ENG, RU, ES

**Eimsbüttel**

UKE University Hospital, Drug and alcohol walk-in clinic, Martinistraße 52, 20246 Hamburg, Phone: 040/ 741054217, Email: drogenambulanz@uke.de, open 24/7, Interpreters for most languages can be arranged.

Frauenperspektiven Substance abuse counselling for women, Charlottenstraße 26, 20257 Hamburg, Phone: 040/ 4329600,

Email: beratungsstelle@frauenperspektiven.de, Mon, Wed & Thu: 10 a.m. - 4 p.m., Fri: 10 a.m. - 2 p.m., ENG

M.A.T. West, Elbgaustraße 83, 22523 Hamburg, Phone: 040/ 57193131, Email: mat-west@therapiehilfe.de, ENG, FA

Hamburg Mitte (Centre)

Büro für Suchtprävention, Repsoldstraße 4, 20097 Hamburg, Phone: 040/ 2849918-24, Email: hls@sucht-hamburg.de, Interpreters for most languages can be arranged.

Drob Inn St. Georg Directed specifically at opiate users, Besenbinderhof 71, 20097 Hamburg, Phone: 040/ 3999930, Email: drob.inn@jugendhilfe.de, Mon, Wed, Thu & Fri: 9 a.m. - 5 p.m., Tue: 2:30 p.m. - 5 p.m., Sat: 12 p.m. - 5 p.m.

KODROBS Wilhelmsburg, Weimarer Straße 83-85, 21107 Hamburg, Phone: 040/ 7216038/ -39, Email:

wilhelmsburg@kodrobs.de, Mon, Tue & Thu: 10 a.m. - 7 p.m., Fri: 10 a.m. - 4 p.m., ENG, RU, KU, TR

Viva Billstedt - Take Care! Substance abuse counselling for young adults, Ruhmkoppel 14, 22119, Phone: 040/ 707020020 or 0151/ 59278822, Email: takecare-billstedt@jugendhilfe.de, open upon request, ENG

Hamburg Nord (North)

MobS Hamburg Nord Substance abuse counselling for young adults, Wischhöfen 1, 22415 Hamburg, Phone: 040/ 55440753, Email: mobs-nord@therapiehilfe.de, open upon request, ENG, RU, POL, FA

Harburg

OkayM.A.T. & Seehaus Harburg, Schlossmühlendamm 8-10, 21073 Hamburg, Phone: 040/ 7679490, Email: mat-harburg@therapiehilfe.de, Mon & Thu: 2 p.m. - 4 p.m., ENG, FA

**STZ Harburg, Knoopstraße 37, 21073 Hamburg, Phone: 040/ 3347533-0, Email: lars.ehricke@martha-stiftung.de, Mon, Wed & Thu: 10 a.m. - 6 p.m., Tue: 2 p.m. - 6 p.m., Fri: 10 a.m. - 3 p.m., ENG, ESP**

**MobS Therapiehilfe**, Cuxhavener Straße 386, 21149 Hamburg, Phone: 040/ 30384444, Email: mobs-harburg@therapiehilfe.de, open upon request, **ENG, POL, RU**

# Wandsbek

**Die Boje Suchthilfe**, Brauhausstieg 15-17, 22041 Hamburg, Phone: 040/ 444091 or 040/ 7314949, Email: beratung@dieboje.de, Mon - Fri: 10 a.m. - 6 p.m., **ENG**

**Die Brücke Eilbek**, Conventstraße 14, 22089 Hamburg, Phone: 040/ 6683638, Tue: 3 p.m. - 5 p.m., **ENG**

**Die Brücke Wandsbek**, Walddörferstraße 337, 22047 Hamburg, Phone: 040/ 6683637, Email: info@ambulante-suchttherapie.de, Tue: 5 p.m. - 7 p.m., Thu: 3 p.m. - 5 p.m., **ENG, ESP**

**Viva Wandsbek - Take Care!** Substance abuse counselling for young adults, Bei den Höfen 23, 22043 Hamburg, Phone: 040/ 244242590 or 0177/ 2094549, Email: takecare@jugendhilfe.de, Mon - Wed: 10 a.m. - 6 p.m., Thu & Fri: 1 p.m. 6 p.m., **ENG**

**Therapeutische Gemeinschaft Jenfeld (TGJ)**, Jenfelder Straße 100, 22045 Hamburg, Phone: 040/ 65409628, Email: info.aha@alida.de, Mon & Thu: 3 p.m. - 5 p.m., **ENG**

# Australia

The phone service is available 24/ by calling (08) **9442 5000** or **1800 198 024** (toll-free for country callers).

**Live Chat** is also free of charge and available for Western Australian residents Monday to Friday 7.30am - 9pm, Saturday 9am - 7pm and

Sunday 11am - 6pm. Live Chat can be accessed here[1].

Email: alcoholdrugsupport@mhc.wa.gov.au

Web: alcoholdrugsupport.mhc.wa.gov.au[2]

---

1. https://www.mhc.wa.gov.au/about-us/our-services/alcohol-and-drug-support-service/live-chat-with-an-alcoholdrug-counsellor/

2. http://alcoholdrugsupport.mhc.wa.gov.au/

# South African

**<u>Elim Clinic (Drug Abuse Treatment Centre)</u>**
– **Call:** 011 975 2951 **(Get Hours)**
– **Website:** www.elimclin.co.za[1]

---

1. http://www.elimclin.co.za/

# United States of America

DrugAbuse.com[1] hotline: Addiction Navigators on call 24/7 to help answer any questions related to drug abuse and support

- Al-Anon[2] and Ala-teen[3] hotline line: 800-356-9996 – Counselors provide support to teens and adults who are negatively impacted by alcohol addiction and provide resources to group therapy nearby for ongoing support.
- Substance Abuse and Mental Health Services Administration[4] (SAMHSA): 1-800-662-4357 – English/Spanish speaking counselors provide referrals to treatment facilities, support groups, and community-based services.
- National Suicide Prevention[5]: 1-800-273-8255 – Support to help those in crisis process their emotional distress and prevent suicide.
- Boys Town[6]: 1-800-448-3000 – Over 140 languages

---

1. https://drugabuse.com/addiction/drug-abuse/hotlines/

2. https://al-anon.org/

3. https://al-anon.org/newcomers/teen-corner-alateen/

4. https://www.samhsa.gov/find-help/national-helpline

5. https://suicidepreventionlifeline.org/

can be translated; they also provide a telecommunications device for the deaf (TDD) line for the speech and hearing impaired (1-800-448-1833).

- Drugfree.org[7]: call 855-378-4373 or text 55753 – Counselors provide support and education and guide you to the best course of action.

---

6. https://www.boystown.org/hotline/Pages/default.aspx

7. https://drugfree.org/article/get-one-on-one-help/

# Canada

**Alberta[1] (Addiction Helpline, Alberta Health Services)**
1-866-332-2322
**British Columbia[2] (Alcohol and Drug Information and Referral Service)**
1-800-663-1441
604-660-9382
**Manitoba[3] (Addictions Foundation of Manitoba)**
Adult services: 1-855-662-6605
Youth services: 1-877-710-3999
204-944-6200
**New Brunswick[4] (Addiction Centres, Department of Health)**
506-674-4300
**Newfoundland and Labrador[5] (Addictions Services, Department of Health and Community Services)**
1-888-737-4668
709-729-3658
**Northwest Territories[6] (Department of Health and Social Services)**
1-800-661-0844

---


1. https://www.albertahealthservices.ca/amh/amh.aspx

2. http://www.bc211.ca/help-lines/#adirs

3. http://afm.mb.ca/programs-and-services/

4. http://www.gnb.ca/0378/centers-e.asp

5. https://www.health.gov.nl.ca/health/mentalhealth_committee/mentalhealth/
   treatment_centres.html

6. https://www.hss.gov.nt.ca/en/services/addictions/getting-help-addictions

867-873-7037
**Nova Scotia**[7] **(Mental Health and Addictions Services, Nova Scotia Health Authority)**
1-888-429-8167
**Nunavut**[8] **(Kamatsiaqtut Help Line)**
1-800-265-3333
867-979-3333
**Ontario**[9] **(ConnexOntario)**
1-866-531-2600
**Prince Edward Island**[10] **(Addiction Services, Health PEI)**
1-833-553-6983
902-368-4120
**Quebec**[11] **(Drugs: help and referral)**
1-800-265-2626
514-527-2626
**Saskatchewan**[12] **(HealthLine, Ministry of Health)**
811 or 1-877-800-0002
306-766-6600
**Yukon**[13] **(Mental Wellness and Substance Use Services, Health and Social Services)**
1-866-456-3838 (for Yukon, Nunavut and NWT)
867-456-3838

---

7. http://www.nshealth.ca/mental-health-addictions

8. http://www.nunavuthelpline.ca/

9. http://www.connexontario.ca/

10. http://www.healthpei.ca/addictions

11. http://www.drogue-aidereference.qc.ca/

12. http://www.saskatchewan.ca/residents/health/accessing-health-care-services/healthline

13. http://www.hss.gov.yk.ca/mwsu_communities.php

# Swiss

+41 31 376 04 01
office@infodrog.ch

# Source Reference

https://www.hamburg.com/residents/social/
11823820/addiction/
https://alcoholthinkagain.com.au/help/
https://www.samsosa.org/wp/help-lines/
https://americanaddictioncenters.org/
rehab-guide/alcohol-drug-hotline
https://www.ccsa.ca/addictions-treatment-
helplines-canada
https://www.infodrog.ch/en/

https://en.m.wikipedia.org/wiki/
National_Suicide_Prevention_Lifeline

https://www.lifeline.org.au[1]
https://www.usa.gov/federal-agencies/office-
on-violence-against-women
https://www.respect.gov.au/services/

https://www.dawncanada.net/issues/
crisis-hotlines/

---

1. https://www.lifeline.org.au

https://www.admin.ch/gov/en/start/
documentation/
media-releases.msg-id-78545.html

https://help.unhcr.org/southafrica/get-help/
violence/
https://www.childhelp.org/contact/
http://worldhelplines.org/canada.html
https://home.crin.org/child-helplines-a-global-
list
Canva

# About The Author

Lesiba Ignitiuas Kekana is also known by his stage name Kevin Kekana. He is born in South Africa( Limpopo in a small town called Mokopane). He is born on 25 October 1998. He is also using his pen name (Kevin Rabalao)as a brand to write small project books. In 2019 he wrote 4 books and he decided to take them down from the retailers because he felt like they are not good enough to be in his bookstore. He believes he is the most gifted author that ever walked on earth. His goal is to create the biggest online library with his 2 author brand names. He can write non-friction and friction books. He enjoys most, writing stories and educating others about his discoveries and research. His logo and signature is #IamKevinGotTheMainIdea

.

# Copyright

[Appreciate me:I need you & I need your Love]
by [Lesiba Ignitiuas Kekana]
Published by [Garther Publishing]

www.ingramcontent.com/pod-product-compliance
Lightning Source LLC
Chambersburg PA
CBHW031442130726
47989CB00003B/1254